Must-Have Oatm

Oat so Simple Recipes for Breakfast & Beyond

BY

Christina Tosch

Copyright Notes

This Book may not be reproduced, in part or in whole, without explicit permission and agreement by the Author by any means. This includes but is not limited to print, electronic media, scanning, photocopying or file sharing.

The Author has made every effort to ensure accuracy of information in the Book but assumes no responsibility should personal or commercial damage arise in the case of misinterpretation or misunderstanding. All suggestions, instructions and guidelines expressed in the Book are meant for informational purposes only, and the Reader assumes any and all risk when following said information.

Table of Contents

Introduction.. 6

Breakfast Oatmeal... 8

Banana Stovetop Oatmeal 9

Banana, Strawberry and Rhubarb Baked Oatmeal.................................... 11

Berry and Banana Baked Oatmeal 14

Black Forest Oatmeal 17

Caramelized Pear Topped Oatmeal 19

Cherry Almond Overnight Oats 21

Chocolate and Raspberry Cheesecake Overnight Oatmeal....................... 23

Chocolate Sea Salt Protein Oatmeal... 25

Cookie Dough Microwave Oatmeal... 27

Earl Grey Oatmeal... 29

Lemon Blueberry Baked Oatmeal.. 31

Peanut Butter Banana Oatmeal Bake 34

Peppermint Mocha Oatmeal.. 37

Pumpkin Baked Oatmeal... 39

Rose Vanilla Oatmeal with Raspberry Jam..42

Southern-Style Bananas Foster Oatmeal..44

Spiced Orange-Hazelnut Oatmeal..47

Totally Tropical Oatmeal..49

Turkish Delight Oats..51

Two-Minute Honey Almond Oatmeal..53

Sweet Oatmeal Snacks and Treats..55

Apple Cinnamon Oatmeal Cookies..56

Brown Butter Chocolate Chip Zucchini Oatmeal Cups..59

Brown Sugar Oatmeal Pancakes..62

Carrot Cake Baked Oatmeal Muffins..64

Chocolate-Dipped Peppermint Oatmeal Cookies..67

Cinnamon Oatmeal Truffles..70

Coconut Oat Muffins..72

Oatmeal Ice Cream..75

Raspberry Oatmeal Popsicles..77

White Chocolate Oatmeal Cranberry Cookies..79

Drinks..82

Avocado Orange Oatmeal Smoothie 83

Chocolate Oat Shake 85

Coffee, Oat, and Banana Smoothie 87

Gingerbread Oatmeal Smoothie 89

Oat Milk 91

Pineapple Coconut Milk Oatmeal Smoothie 93

Pomegranate Blueberry Oatmeal Smoothie 95

Strawberry Oatmeal Smoothie 97

Vanilla Peppermint Overnight Oatmeal Smoothie 99

Vanilla Oatmeal Latte 101

Author's Afterthoughts 103

About the Author 104

Introduction

Old-fashioned, quick-cooking, and rolled – there are many different types of oats to choose from, but one thing for sure, oats are a real must-have superfood!

By including oatmeal in your daily diet, you are adding a valuable grain to your eating plan.

Oats are an excellent source of fiber, which will help keep you fuller for longer and assist with weight loss. They are filled with vitamins, minerals, and antioxidants which can help to regulate blood pressure levels.

The good news is, you can enjoy oats every day, and they are especially *oat-standing* to serve at breakfast time. As we all know, the first meal of the day is the most important. Your body which has fasted for around 8 hours or more, wakes up and needs fuel to power it through the day ahead.

A great way to provide all of the important must-have energy is by serving up a portion of oatmeal. Here you can add plant milk, fruit, nuts, seeds, and natural sweeteners such as honey and maple syrup and create a meal that is healthy and flavorful.

And it doesn't end there! You can not only add oats to smoothies but also in sweet snacks and treat recipes too.

If you are searching for a must-have oatmeal recipe, you have come to the right place! Discover 40 Oat So Simple Recipes for Breakfast & Beyond.

Breakfast Oatmeal

Banana Stovetop Oatmeal

Wake up to the best-ever breakfast and start the day with this fluffy and sweet stovetop oatmeal.

Servings: 2

Total Time: 15mins

Ingredients:

- 1 cup rolled oat
- 2½ cups almond milk, unsweetened and divided
- 2 tbsp pure maple syrup
- 1 banana, peeled and mashed
- 1 tsp vanilla extract
- ½ tsp ground cinnamon
- 1 tbsp chia seeds
- Chopped Walnuts to serve
- Fresh banana slices to serve

Directions:

Add the rolled oats, 2 cups of milk, maple syrup, banana, vanilla extract, ground cinnamon, and chia seeds to a pan. On high to moderate heat, mix to combine and bring to a boil.

Reduce the heat to low-moderate and simmer for approximately 5 minutes, stirring continually until the oatmeal thickens.

Add the remaining milk and stir to combine. Allow to simmer for another 1-2 minutes.

Serve topped with chopped walnuts and slices of fresh banana.

Banana, Strawberry and Rhubarb Baked Oatmeal

Fiber and protein-rich oatmeal filled with fresh fruit is a healthy yet flavorful morning meal and goes a long way to making sure you and your family get their 5-a-day.

Servings: 6

Total Time: 45mins

Ingredients:

- Nonstick coconut oil baking spray
- 1 cup fresh rhubarb, trimmed and chopped into bite-size pieces
- ¼ cup honey
- 1 ripe banana
- 2 eggs
- 1 tsp vanilla extract
- ¾ cup almond milk, unsweetened
- 2 cups old fashioned rolled oats
- ½ cup oat flour
- 1 tsp baking powder
- 1 cup fresh strawberries, hulled and chopped
- A pinch of salt
- A handful of strawberries, hulled and sliced

Directions:

Preheat the main oven to 350 degrees F. Spritz a 10x7" baking dish with nonstick coconut oil baking spray.

Add the chopped rhubarb to a bowl, and add the honey. Mix thoroughly and put to one side while you prepare the remaining ingredients.

Add the banana to a second bowl, and with a metal fork, mash to a puree.

Add the eggs, vanilla extract, almond milk, and mix until incorporated.

Next, add the rolled oats, oat flour, baking powder, chopped strawberries, and a pinch of salt. Mix well to combine.

Spoon the batter into the prepared baking dish. Then, using a spatula, spread out evenly.

Top the oatmeal with slices of strawberries and bake in the preheated oven for 35-40 minutes until the oatmeal is firm to the touch.

Allow to cool slightly before serving.

Berry and Banana Baked Oatmeal

Breakfast or brunch, you can't go wrong with this sweet yet healthy baked oatmeal.

Servings: 6

Total Time: 35mins

Ingredients:

- Nonstick coconut oil baking spray
- 1 large ripe banana, peeled
- 2 large eggs
- 1 tsp vanilla extract
- ¼ cup pure maple syrup
- ½ cup unsweetened almond milk
- 2 tbsp coconut oil, melted
- 2 cups old fashioned rolled oats
- ½ cup white whole wheat flour
- 1 cup fresh berries of choice
- 1 tsp baking powder
- 1 tsp cinnamon

Directions:

Preheat the main oven to 350 degrees F. Using nonstick spray, spritz an 8" square baking dish.

Add the banana to a bowl, and with a metal fork, mash to a smooth puree.

Add the eggs, vanilla extract, syrup, almond milk, coconut oil, rolled oats, flour, berries, baking powder, and cinnamon to the mashed banana. Mix thoroughly until combined.

Spoon the batter into the prepared dish and bake for 30 minutes at 350 degrees F until the surface starts to brown.

Remove from the oven. Then, allow to cool.

Serve and enjoy.

Black Forest Oatmeal

If you have a sweet tooth, this decadent oatmeal with dried cherries, topped with whipped cream and chocolate chips, is a bountiful breakfast dish or sensational supper snack.

Servings: 4

Total Time: 25mins

Ingredients:

- 3¾ cups water, divided
- ¼ tsp salt
- 2 cups old-fashioned oats
- ¼ cup toasted wheat germ
- ½ cup baking cocoa
- ⅓ cup sugar
- 2 tsp vanilla extract
- 1 cup + dried cherries
- Miniature semi-sweet chocolate chips to serve
- Sweetened whipped cream to serve

Directions:

In a large pan, bring 3¼ cups of water and salt to a boil.

Stir in the oats and toasted wheat germ and turn the heat down. Uncovered, simmer for 5 minutes until the water is absorbed.

In the meantime, combine the baking cocoa with the sugar, vanilla extract, and remaining ½ cup of water and stir well until smooth.

Add the cocoa mixture and 1 cup of dried cherries to the oats, and stir until incorporated and heated through.

Serve the oatmeal with a sprinkling of cherries, mini chocolate chips, and whipped cream.

Caramelized Pear Topped Oatmeal

Sweet quick-cook oats topped with caramelized pears elevate a regular oatmeal dish with a sticky fruit topping.

Servings: 2-3

Total Time: 12mins

Ingredients:

Topping:

- 1 ripe Bartlett pear, rinsed, cored and thinly sliced
- 2 tbsp butter
- 2 tbsp brown sugar
- ½ tsp ground cinnamon

Oatmeal:

- ½ cup quick-cook oats
- Brown sugar to taste, as needed
- 2 tbsp chopped walnuts for topping

Directions:

For the caramelized pears: In a pan over moderate heat, combine the pears with the butter, and while stirring occasionally, cook for 1-2 minutes until the pears are coated in the butter and fork-tender.

Add the brown sugar and stir to coat the pears. Cook for an additional 60 seconds until a caramel sauce starts to form. Scatter over the ground cinnamon, fold gently to coat the pears, and remove the pan from the heat.

For the oatmeal, cook the oats according to the package instructions.

Stir in brown sugar if needed to sweeten.

Spoon the oats into bowls, top with caramelized pears and nuts, and enjoy immediately.

Cherry Almond Overnight Oats

This dairy-free oatmeal is a convenient make-ahead breakfast dish and the perfect healthy meal to welcome a new day.

Servings: 2

Total Time: 4hrs 10mins

Ingredients:

- 2 cups almond milk, unsweetened
- 2 tbsp honey
- 1 tsp vanilla extract
- A pinch of sea salt
- 1 cup old fashioned oats
- 1 tbsp chia seeds
- ¼ cup slivered almonds
- 1 cup fresh cherries, pitted and halved
- Toppings (optional):
- Slivered almonds
- Honey to drizzle
- Fresh cherries, pitted and quartered

Directions:

In a bowl, whisk the milk with the honey, vanilla extract, and sea salt.

Stir in the oats, chia seeds, almonds, and fresh cherries until combined.

Cover the bowl. Then, transfer to the fridge for 4 hours.

Serve the oatmeal topped with almonds, a drizzle of honey, and fresh cherries.

Chocolate and Raspberry Cheesecake Overnight Oatmeal

If you know you have a busy day ahead, it's a good idea to plan breakfast for the following morning by preparing a bowl of this overnight oatmeal.

Servings: 2

Total Time: 8hrs 12mins

Ingredients:

- 1 cup old fashioned rolled oats
- 1 tbsp chia seeds
- 3 tbsp cocoa powder
- A pinch of salt
- 1 cup almond milk, unsweetened
- ½ cup plain Greek yogurt
- 3 tbsp maple syrup
- 1 tsp vanilla extract
- ½ cup fresh raspberries, divided
- Greek yogurt to serve

Directions:

Add the rolled oats, chia seeds, cocoa powder, a pinch of salt, almond milk, Greek yogurt, maple syrup, and vanilla extract to a bowl, and mix until incorporated.

Cover the bowl, and transfer to the fridge overnight.

The following day, remove the oats from the fridge.

Add half of the fresh raspberries to a bowl and mash with a fork. Add the mashed berries to the oatmeal and stir and swirl to combine.

Serve the oatmeal with a dollop of Greek yogurt and a scattering of the remaining fresh raspberries.

Chocolate Sea Salt Protein Oatmeal

When you don't have a lot of time on your hands, enjoy a bowl of this high-protein oatmeal.

Servings: 2

Total Time: 15mins

Ingredients:

- 1 cup rolled oats
- 2 cups almond milk, unsweetened
- 1 tbsp ground flaxseed
- 1 tbsp chia seeds
- 4 tbsp chocolate protein powder any brand
- 2 tbsp dark cocoa powder
- 1 tbsp + almond butter
- A pinch of ground cinnamon
- A pinch of salt
- Coconut sugar to taste, as needed
- Sea salt to serve

Directions:

In a saucepan, combine the rolled oats with the milk, flaxseed, chia seeds, chocolate protein powder, dark cocoa powder, 1 tablespoon of almond butter, ground cinnamon, and a pinch of salt.

Over high heat, and while stirring continuously, bring the mixture to a boil. Once at a boil, turn the heat down to low and continue stirring for approximately 4-5 minutes. The oats are ready when they are thickened to your preferred consistency. Sweeten with coconut sugar to taste.

Serve the oatmeal with a knob of almond butter and a sprinkling of sea salt.

Cookie Dough Microwave Oatmeal

Just because you are in a hurry, it doesn't mean you have to forgo a tasty breakfast, and thanks to your trusty microwave, this sweet oatmeal is good to go in just five minutes.

Servings: 1

Total Time: 5mins

Ingredients:

- ½ cup rolled oats
- ⅔ cup unsweetened almond milk
- ½ tbsp nut butter of choice
- 2 tsp pure maple syrup
- ½ tbsp mini chocolate chips to serve

Directions:

In a microwave-safe bowl, combine the rolled oats with almond milk, nut butter (of choice), and maple syrup.

In a microwave, cook on high for 60 seconds.

Stir the oatmeal and return to the microwave, and cook for an additional 60 seconds. Then, remove from the microwave and stir once more.

Allow to cool for a couple of minutes before sprinkling over the mini chocolate chips.

Earl Grey Oatmeal

Tea for two! But not served in a cup, instead use Earl Grey teabags to infuse and add the flavor to a satisfying bowl of this breakfast oatmeal.

Servings: 2

Total Time: 25mins

Ingredients:

- 1 cup water
- 1 cup milk
- 2 Earl Grey tea bags
- 1 cup rolled oats
- 1 tbsp honey
- Splash of milk to serve
- Honey to serve, optional
- Fresh blackberries to serve

Directions:

In a pot, combine the water with the milk and bring it to a bare simmer. Remove the pot from the heat, add the Earl Grey tea bags, and steep for 10 minutes.

Return the pot to the heat source. Add the oats, bringing to a simmer while frequently stirring. Then, allow the mixture to simmer for around 5-10 minutes until the oats start to soften and the liquid absorbs. Remove and discard the tea bags.

Stir in 1 tablespoon of honey and spoon into bowls.

Serve with a splash of milk, a drizzle of honey, and a sprinkling of fresh berries.

Lemon Blueberry Baked Oatmeal

In less than one hour, you and your family could be tucking into a bowl of this citrus and berry baked oatmeal. So what are you waiting for?

Servings: 8

Total Time: 40mins

Ingredients:

- Nonstick coconut oil baking spray
- 1 ripe medium banana, peeled
- 2 cups blueberries, divided
- ¼ cup honey
- 1 tsp vanilla extract
- ½ cup almond milk, unsweetened
- 2 cups old fashioned rolled oats
- ½ cup white whole wheat flour
- 1 tsp baking powder
- A pinch of salt
- 2 large eggs
- 1 cup fresh blueberries, divided
- Zest of 1 lemon
- Greek yogurt to serve, optional

Directions:

Preheat the main oven to 350 degrees F. Spritz a 10x7" baking dish with nonstick coconut oil baking spray.

Add the banana, 1 cup of blueberries, honey, vanilla extract, and milk to a blender or processor and process to a puree.

Transfer the mixture to a bowl. Add the rolled oats followed by the flour, baking powder, and a pinch of salt. Then, mix to combine. Add the eggs and mix once more.

Finally, add ¾ cup of fresh blueberries and lemon zest and mix to combine.

Spoon the batter into the baking dish, and with a spatula, spread it out evenly. Scatter the remaining blueberries over the top.

Bake the oatmeal in the oven until firm to the touch, for approximately 30 minutes.

Serve with a dollop of Greek yogurt.

Peanut Butter Banana Oatmeal Bake

Peanut butter is a versatile ingredient, but instead of using it as a sandwich filling, why not add it to a bowl of comforting oatmeal?

Servings: 4

Total Time: 35mins

Ingredients:

- Nonstick coconut oil baking spray
- 1 ripe banana, peeled
- 2 large eggs
- ⅓ cup smooth peanut butter
- 1 tsp vanilla extract
- 2 tbsp pure maple syrup
- ½ cup almond milk, unsweetened
- 1½ cups rolled oats
- ¼ cup oat flour
- 1 tsp baking powder
- A pinch of salt
- 1 banana, peeled and sliced

Directions:

Preheat the main oven to 375 degrees F. Spritz a 9" square cake pan or baking dish with cooking spray.

In a bowl, mash the banana with a metal fork until a puree.

Add the eggs, peanut butter, vanilla extract, maple syrup, and milk, mixing until silky smooth.

Next, add the rolled oats, followed by the baking powder and salt. Mix well to combine entirely.

Then, spoon the batter into the prepared pan or dish.

Add a few slices of banana over the surface of the batter.

Bake the oatmeal in the oven for approximately 30-40 minutes, until firm to the touch.

Serve and enjoy.

Peppermint Mocha Oatmeal

Enjoy a taste of the holidays all-year-round with this festive flavor oatmeal.

Servings: 1

Total Time: 10mins

Ingredients:

- ⅔ cup strong brewed coffee
- ⅓ cup milk of choice
- ½ cup old fashioned oats
- 2 tsp pure maple syrup
- 1 tbsp cocoa powder, unsweetened
- 3-4 drops peppermint extract
- ¼ cup coconut yogurt for topping
- ½ tbsp crushed candy canes for topping

Directions:

In a small pan, heat the strong brewed coffee with the milk.

Add the oats and maple syrup and bring to a boil. Reduce the heat and simmer while occasionally stirring for 4-5 minutes.

Stir in the cocoa powder.

Remove the pan from the heat. Then, stir in the peppermint extract.

Spoon the oatmeal into a bowl. Top with coconut yogurt and scatter over crushed candy canes.

Pumpkin Baked Oatmeal

Enjoy all the flavors of fall, all-year-round, in this hearty baked oatmeal dish topped with mini chocolate chips.

Servings: 6

Total Time: 40mins

Ingredients:

- Nonstick coconut oil baking spray
- 1½ cups old fashioned rolled oats
- ½ cup white whole wheat flour
- 1 tsp pumpkin pie spice
- 1 tsp baking powder
- A pinch of salt
- 2 large eggs
- ½ cup almond milk, unsweetened
- ¾ cup pumpkin puree, unsweetened
- 1 tsp vanilla extract
- 3 tbsp pure maple syrup
- ½ cup mini choc chips to serve

Directions:

Preheat the main oven to 350 degrees F. Spritz a 9" square baking dish with nonstick baking spray.

Add the rolled oats, flour, pumpkin pie spice, baking powder, and salt to a bowl and mix well to combine.

Next, add the eggs, almond milk, pumpkin puree, vanilla extract, maple syrup, and combine well.

Then, spoon the batter into the prepared baking dish, and using a spatula, spread it out evenly.

Scatter the mini choc chips over the oatmeal's surface and bake in the preheated oven for approximately 25 minutes until firm to the touch.

Remove the oatmeal from the oven, and allow to cool for a minimum of 10 minutes before enjoying.

Rose Vanilla Oatmeal with Raspberry Jam

Treat yourself to this delicate tasting oatmeal which is ready to enjoy in just 5 minutes.

Servings: 1

Total Time: 5mins

Ingredients:

- ½ cup old fashioned oats
- 1 cup milk
- ½ tsp vanilla extract
- 1 tsp rose water
- 1 tsp sugar
- A pinch of salt
- 1 tsp raspberry jam
- Fresh raspberries to serve

Directions:

In a microwave-safe bowl, combine the oats, vanilla extract, milk, rose water, sugar, and salt.

On high, microwave for 3-4 minutes until the oatmeal is your preferred consistency.

Swirl in the raspberry jam, and top with fresh raspberries.

Serve warm, and enjoy.

Southern-Style Bananas Foster Oatmeal

Let the good times roll with this healthy version of New Orleans's favorite dessert, Bananas Foster.

Servings: 4

Total Time: 15mins

Ingredients:

- 2 cups water
- 1½ cups 2% milk
- ½ tsp salt
- 2 cups old-fashioned oats
- ½ cup butter, cubed
- ½ cup packed brown sugar
- ½ tsp ground cinnamon
- A pinch of ground ginger
- A pinch of ground nutmeg
- 2 medium firm-ripe bananas, peeled and sliced
- ½ tsp rum extract
- ½ tsp vanilla extract

Optional Toppings:

- Cinnamon sugar
- Fresh banana Slices
- Whipped cream

Directions:

In a large pan, bring the water, milk, and salt to a boil.

Stir in the oats, and over moderate heat, cook for 5 minutes while occasionally stirring. Cover the pan with a lid, and allow to stand.

In a small pan, over moderate heat, melt the butter.

Next, stir in the cinnamon, brown sugar, ginger, and nutmeg, and bring to a boil.

Turn the heat down and uncovered, simmer until slightly thickened, for 5 minutes.

Add the bananas, and while stirring, gently cook until the bananas are softened slightly and glazed for 1-2 minutes.

Then, remove the pan from the heat and stir in the rum and vanilla extracts.

Stir the banana mixture into the oatmeal and serve with your favorite toppings.

Spiced Orange-Hazelnut Oatmeal

Cardamom and ginger-infused whipped cream, fresh fruit, and crunchy nuts are the perfect spiced toppings for this texture-rich oatmeal.

Servings: 4

Total Time: 25mins

Ingredients:

- ½ cup heavy whipping cream
- 2 tsp sugar
- ⅛ tsp ground cardamom
- 1 tbsp crystallized ginger, finely chopped
- 3¼ cups water
- ¼ tsp salt
- 2 cups old fashioned oats
- 8 dates, pitted and chopped
- 1½ cups orange segments, seeded
- ½ cup hazelnuts, chopped and toasted

Directions:

In a bowl, beat the cream until it starts to thicken.

Add the sugar and ground cardamom to the cream, and beat until soft peaks begin to form.

Stir in the chopped ginger.

In a large pan, bring the water along with the salt to a boil.

Stir in the oats and chopped dates, and over moderate heat, cook for 5 minutes while occasionally stirring.

Transfer the oatmeal to bowls and top with the orange segments, spiced whipped cream, and chopped hazelnuts.

Serve and enjoy.

Totally Tropical Oatmeal

Enjoy a taste of Tropics without leaving your home. Here, coconut and fresh fruit come together to deliver a bountiful bowl of this oatmeal.

Servings: 1

Total Time: 20mins

Ingredients:

- 1½ ounces old fashioned oats
- 1 cup coconut milk
- ½ tbsp coconut butter
- Grated coconut, fresh or desiccated as needed
- ½ fresh mango, pitted and coarsely chopped
- 2 slices fresh pineapple, peeled, cored and chopped
- 1 passion fruit, cut in half

Directions:

Prepare the oats and coconut milk according to the package directions.

In the meantime, prepare the topping.

When the oats are cooked, add the coconut butter and stir in some grated coconut.

Spoon the oats into a bowl, top with the fresh mango and pineapple, and garnish with more grated coconut.

Squeeze the passion fruit seeds from ½ of the passion fruit over the surface of the oatmeal. Spoon the flesh out of the other passion fruit half and serve on the side.

Turkish Delight Oats

Add a little Eastern promise to your diet with this fragrant oat dish. It not only tastes good, but it also looks sensational.

Servings: 1

Total Time: 21hrs

Ingredients:

- 1½ ounces rolled oats
- 1 cup plant-based milk of choice
- 1-2 tsp rose syrup to taste
- 2-4 cubes dark chocolate
- A small handful of pistachios, crushed
- A small handful of pomegranate arils
- Cacao nibs to serve
- Edible rose petals to serve

Directions:

Add the rolled oats and milk and cook according to the package directions. This will take 10-12 minutes on the stovetop.

In the meantime, prepare the toppings.

Once the oats are cooked, stir in the rose syrup to taste.

Spoon approximately half of the oats into a bowl. Then, add a cube or two of dark chocolate to the oats, and top with the remaining oats.

Top with another 1-2 cubes of chocolate, followed by the pistachios, pomegranate arils, cacao nibs, and edible rose petals.

Two-Minute Honey Almond Oatmeal

All you need to prepare this oatmeal is a microwave, its four ingredients, and its recipe, and hey presto, you have a healthy breakfast!

Servings: 1

Total Time: 2mins

Ingredients:

- ½ cup rolled oats
- ½ cup skim milk
- 1 tsp almond butter, unsalted
- 1 tsp runny honey

Directions:

In a bowl, combine the rolled oats with milk, almond butter, and honey, and microwave for 60 seconds.

Stir, microwave for an additional 60 seconds, stir and serve.

Sweet Oatmeal Snacks and Treats

Apple Cinnamon Oatmeal Cookies

These soft and chewy cookies won't last long! Serve them as a sweet snack with your morning coffee or with a glass of milk at supper time.

Servings: 20

Total Time: 20mins

Ingredients:

- Nonstick coconut oil baking spray
- 1½ cups quick-cook oats
- 1 cup white whole wheat flour
- ½ tsp baking powder
- 1½ tsp ground cinnamon
- 1 cup packed brown sugar
- A pinch of salt
- 1 cup applesauce, unsweetened
- ¾ cup fresh Gala apple, cored and diced
- 1 large egg
- 1 tsp vanilla extract
- 1½ tbsp coconut oil, melted
- Cored and diced Gala apple for topping
- Ground cinnamon to dust

Directions:

Preheat the main oven to 350 degrees F. Spritz a baking sheet with nonstick coconut oil baking spray.

Add the oats, whole wheat flour, baking powder, 1½ teaspoons of ground cinnamon, brown sugar, a pinch of salt to a bowl, and combine.

In a second bowl, combine the applesauce with the diced apples, egg, and vanilla extract. Whisk well.

Add the applesauce mixture to the rolled oat mixture, and mix once more.

Lastly, add the coconut oil, and mix to combine to create a batter that is a thinner consistency than regular cookie dough.

Using a 1½ tablespoon cookie scoop, transfer the batter onto the prepared baking sheets. Using clean hands, flatten the cookie dough.

Top each cookie with a little diced apple.

Bake in the preheated oven for 12-15 minutes until the bottoms start to brown.

Remove the cookies from the oven. Then, transfer them to a cooling rack.

Dust with ground cinnamon and serve.

Brown Butter Chocolate Chip Zucchini Oatmeal Cups

If you are looking for a healthy snack on-the-move, then these oatmeal cups are ideal. Pop one or two of them in your lunch box, and you are good to go!

Servings: 12

Total Time: 30mins

Ingredients:

- Nonstick coconut oil baking spray
- 3 cups rolled oats
- 1 tsp baking powder
- 1 cup zucchini, shredded and squeezed of liquid
- 1 tsp ground cinnamon
- 3 tbsp unsalted butter
- 2 large eggs
- ½ cup applesauce, unsweetened
- 1 cup milk of choice
- ½ cup mini chocolate chips

Directions:

Preheat the main oven to 350 degrees F. Using nonstick baking spray, spritz 2 (6-cup) muffin pans.

Add the rolled oats, baking powder, zucchini, and ground cinnamon to a bowl, and combine. Set to one side.

Next, over moderate to high heat, melt the butter in a small pan. Once the butter is caramelized, turn the heat off and allow the pan to sit until the butter is browned.

Add the browned butter to the dry ingredients and add the shredded zucchini mixture, butter, eggs, applesauce, eggs, and milk. Mix thoroughly to combine and fold in the chocolate chips.

Transfer the batter to the prepared muffin cups to approximately 75 percent full.

Bake in the preheated oven for 20-25 minutes, until springy to the touch.

Remove from the oven and cool for 4-6 minutes before transferring to a cooling rack to cool fully.

Brown Sugar Oatmeal Pancakes

When the weekend comes around, why not whip up a batch of these sweet brown sugar oatmeal pancakes?

Servings: 8-10

Total Time: 15mins

Ingredients:

- ½ cup + 2 tbsp quick-cook oats
- ½ cup whole wheat flour
- ½ cup all-purpose flour
- ½ tsp bicarbonate of soda
- ½ tsp salt
- ⅓ cup packed brown sugar
- 1 large egg, room temperature
- 2 tbsp vegetable oil
- 1 cup buttermilk
- Fresh chopped fruit of choice to serve

Directions:

In a bowl, combine the oats with whole wheat flour, all-purpose flour, bicarbonate of soda, salt, and brown sugar.

In a second smaller bowl, beat the egg with the vegetable oil and buttermilk.

Stir the oat mixture into the egg mixture until just moistened.

In ⅓ cupfuls, pour the batter on a greased hot griddle. Flip the batter over once bubbles start to form on the surface, and cook until the underside is golden.

Top with your favorite fresh fruit.

Carrot Cake Baked Oatmeal Muffins

Snacking on sweet food doesn't always have to be unhealthy, as these carrot cake baked oatmeal muffins prove.

Servings: 12

Total Time: 30mins

Ingredients:

- 2 ripe bananas, peeled
- ¼ cup almond butter
- 1½ cups old-fashioned oats
- ¾ cup milk
- ⅛ cup honey
- ½ tsp vanilla extract
- ¼ tsp kosher salt
- 1 egg
- 1 tsp baking powder
- ¾ cup carrots, grated
- 1½ tsp cinnamon
- ½ cup raisins
- ¼ cup pecans, chopped

Directions:

Preheat the main oven to 375 degrees F. Line 12 muffin cups with parchment paper.

To prepare the muffins: In a bowl, mash the bananas. Add the almond butter, oats, milk, honey, vanilla extract, kosher salt, egg, and baking powder, and stir with a whisk.

In a bowl, combine the grated carrots with the cinnamon, raisins, and pecans and add the mixture to the previous step's muffin mixture.

Next, evenly divide the batter between the prepared muffin cups.

Bake in the preheated oven for 20-30 minutes, until springy to the touch.

Remove from the oven. Then, allow the muffins to cool while still in the pan for 5 minutes.

Then, remove from the pan and allow to cool completely.

Serve and enjoy.

Chocolate-Dipped Peppermint Oatmeal Cookies

Spoil your family and friends with these scrumptious white chocolate dipped peppermint oatmeal cookies.

Servings: 24

Total Time: 35mins

Ingredients:

- 1 cup butter
- 1 cup brown sugar
- 1 cup sugar
- 1 tsp vanilla extract
- 2 eggs
- 1½ cups flour
- 1 tsp cream of tartar
- 1 tsp bicarbonate of soda
- 1 tsp salt
- 3 cups old fashioned oats
- 1 cup peppermint baking chips
- 2 cups white chocolate, chopped
- Candy canes, crushed

Directions:

In a bowl, cream the butter with both sugars until fluffy.

Add the vanilla extract and eggs.

Next, in a second bowl, combine the dry ingredients (flour, cream of tartar, bicarb, salt, and oats) and add them to the butter mixture.

Fold in the peppermint baking chips.

Using a cookie scoop, scoop the dough onto baking sheets. You should aim to yield around 24 cookies.

Then, bake the cookies in the oven at 350 degrees F for 10-12 minutes.

Remove from the oven and set aside to cool completely.

When cool, melt the white chocolate.

Dip each cookie into the chocolate to come approximately ⅓ of the way.

Arrange the chocolate-dipped cookies on a cookie sheet lined with parchment paper.

While the chocolate is still wet, scatter over the crushed candy canes, and put aside until set.

Cinnamon Oatmeal Truffles

These truffles featuring oats, nuts, and dates are pop-in-the-mouth perfection.

Servings: 12

Total Time: 20mins

Ingredients:

- 1 cup oats
- ½ cup walnuts
- ¾ tsp cinnamon pie spice
- ¼ tsp salt
- 12 Medjool dates, pitted
- 1 tbsp water

Directions:

In a food processor, process the oats, walnuts, cinnamon pie spice, and salt to the consistency of the ground meal.

Remove the oat mixture from the processor.

In the processor, process the dates until they are broken down and form a paste ball.

Return the oat and nut mixture to the processor, and add the water. Process the mixture until combined thoroughly.

Using clean hands, rolls the mixture into 12 even size balls.

Transfer to the fridge, or enjoy immediately.

Coconut Oat Muffins

Lots of coconut flakes add flavor and texture to these oat muffins. Serve with coffee or tea and enjoy an *oat-standing* snack.

Servings: 15

Total Time: 35mins

Ingredients:

- 1 cup sweetened coconut flakes
- Milk as needed for coconut flakes
- 2 eggs
- ⅓ cup agave nectar
- ¾ cup low-fat buttermilk
- ¼ cup vegetable oil
- 1 tsp vanilla extract
- 1 tsp coconut extract
- 1 cup all-purpose flour
- 2½ tsp baking powder
- ½ tsp bicarbonate of soda
- ¼ tsp salt
- 2 cups old-fashioned oats
- ½ cup sweetened coconut flakes for topping

Directions:

Preheat the main oven to 350 degrees F. Using cupcake liners, line muffin pans.

Add the coconut flakes to a cup and fill the cup with milk. Set aside to soak while you continue with the recipe. You will need to squeeze the milk out before adding the coconut flakes to the batter.

Whisk the eggs with the agave syrup, buttermilk, vegetable oil, vanilla extract, and coconut extract into a bowl. Whisk well until combined.

Using a sieve, sift in the all-purpose flour followed by the baking powder, bicarb of soda, and salt. Whisk thoroughly until the mixture is combined fully.

Mix in the oats along with the prepared coconut flakes from Step 2.

Evenly divide the batter between the muffin cups, filling each one 75 percent full.

Top with the additional 2 cups of coconut flakes and bake in the preheated oven for 18-20 minutes, until springy to the touch.

Set the muffins aside to cool and enjoy.

Oatmeal Ice Cream

It's official. Rolled oats aren't just for breakfast; they are an excellent ingredient for a sweet snack or treat too!

Servings: 4

Total Time: 2hrs 30mins

Ingredients:

- 3 cups light canned coconut milk
- 1½ cups rolled oats
- 10 Medjool dates, pitted
- 1 tsp vanilla extract
- A pinch of salt

Directions:

In a food blender, process the coconut milk, rolled oats, dates, vanilla extract, and salt on high speed for 45-60 seconds, until creamy smooth.

Transfer the mixture into an ice-cream maker and process according to the manufacturer's direction to a soft-serve consistency. This process will take approximately 40 minutes.

Transfer the mixture to a shallow container and place in the freezer for 1-2 hours.

Scoop the ice cream into a bowl and serve.

Raspberry Oatmeal Popsicles

If your little ones like popsicles, then why not make a batch of them using healthy oats and fruit?

Servings: 8

Total Time: 8hrs 10mins

Ingredients:

- ½ cup quick-cook oats
- 1 cup milk of choice
- 1 cup frozen raspberries
- 3 tbsp maple syrup
- ½ cup raspberry yogurt

Directions:

Add the oats and milk to a bowl. In the microwave, heat for 1-2 minutes until it is steaming.

Add the frozen berries and maple syrup to the oatmeal.

Fill 8 popsicle molds with 2-3 spoonfuls of the oatmeal mixture. Next, add a layer of raspberry yogurt. Alternate the ingredients until the molds are filled.

Freeze the popsicles overnight.

White Chocolate Oatmeal Cranberry Cookies

These oatmeal cookies are everything they should be, buttery, warmly spiced, chocolate-filled, soft, and chewy. What more could you want from a sweet snack?

Servings: 24

Total Time: 1hr

Ingredients:

- 1 cup flour
- ½ tsp bicarbonate of soda
- ½ tsp ground cinnamon
- ¼ tsp salt
- ½ cup unsalted butter, softened
- ½ cup light brown sugar
- ¼ cup granulated sugar
- 1 egg, room temperature
- ½ tsp almond extract
- 1½ cups old fashioned rolled oats
- ¾ cup sweetened dried cranberries
- ¾ cup white chocolate chips

Directions:

Whisk the flour with the bicarb, ground cinnamon, and salt into a bowl. Set the bowl to one side.

In a bowl, and using a handheld mixer or a stand mixer bowl plus paddle attachment, beat the butter with both sugars until smooth.

Add the egg and almond extract while scraping down the sides of the bowl as necessary.

A little at a time, add the flour mixture to the egg mixture and mix until combined.

Add the rolled oats, dried cranberries, and white chocolate chips and mix thoroughly until entirely combined.

Cover the dough and transfer it to the fridge for a minimum of 30 minutes.

Preheat the main oven to 350 degrees F. Using parchment paper, line 2 large baking sheets.

With a 1½ -2 cup tablespoon-size cookie scoop, scoop the dough onto the prepared baking sheets.

Then, roll the dough into even size balls and press down gently with your hands to flatten slightly.

In batches, bake in the oven for 10-12 minutes.

Remove from the oven and allow to cool on the baking sheets for 6-8 minutes before transferring to a wire rack to cool completely.

Drinks

Avocado Orange Oatmeal Smoothie

Boost all-important energy levels with this creamy smoothie featuring avocados. They are an excellent source of fiber, folate, and potassium.

Servings: 1

Total Time: 3mins

Ingredients:

- ½ cup rolled oats
- 1 cup vanilla almond milk, unsweetened
- ½ avocado, peeled, pitted and chopped
- 1 fresh orange, peeled and seeded
- 1 cup baby spinach leaves
- 1 tbsp pure maple syrup

Directions:

Add the oats, milk, avocado, orange, spinach leaves, and maple syrup to a food blender and process until smooth for 30-60 seconds.

Transfer to a glass, and enjoy.

Chocolate Oat Shake

Forget calorie-laden shakes and instead opt for this dairy-free version made with unsweetened almond milk.

Servings: 2

Total Time: 3mins

Ingredients:

- ½ cup oats
- 1 tbsp cocoa powder
- 1 tsp vanilla extract
- 8-10 ice cubes
- A pinch of salt
- 1 tbsp maple syrup
- 1 cup almond milk, unsweetened

Directions:

In a blender, combine the oats, cocoa powder, vanilla extract, ice cubes, salt, maple syrup, and process until smooth.

A little at a time, add the almond milk until you achieve your preferred consistency.

Serve and enjoy.

Coffee, Oat, and Banana Smoothie

Get your caffeine shot and breakfast oatmeal all in one glass with this healthy smoothie for two.

Servings: 2

Total Time: 15mins

Ingredients:

- ¼ cup rolled oats
- ½ cup dairy milk, warm
- ½ cup cold-brewed coffee, chilled
- 3 tbsp maple syrup
- 1 ripe banana, peeled and sliced
- 1 cup ice

Directions:

In a bowl, combine the oats with the warmed milk. Set the mixture aside for the oats to soften for 10 minutes.

Add the oat mixture, chilled cold-brewed coffee, maple syrup, banana, and ice to a blender, and process for 60 seconds until smooth.

Serve and enjoy.

Gingerbread Oatmeal Smoothie

Gingerbread is a favorite holiday flavor. Here, ginger and spice add warmth to this oatmeal smoothie.

Servings: 2

Total Time: 5mins

Ingredients:

- 2 cups almond milk, unsweetened
- 2 tbsp chia seeds
- ¼ cup oats
- ¾ tsp ginger
- ¼ tsp mixed spice
- 2 tbsp molasses

Directions:

In a food blender, combine the milk with chia seeds, oats, ginger, mixed spice, and molasses.

Pour the smoothie into 2 chilled glasses and enjoy immediately.

Oat Milk

While you may already be a fan of soy, coconut, and almond milk, you may not have come across another great non-dairy option. The homemade oat milk is thick and creamy and can be used in hot drinks, over cereal, or for baking.

Servings: N/A*

Total Time: 35mins

Ingredients:

- 1 cup rolled oats
- 4 cups water
- ¾ -1 tbsp maple syrup to taste
- ¼ tsp salt

Directions:

In a blender, combine the oats with the water, maple syrup (to taste), and salt and process for approximately 60 seconds.

Using a fine-mesh sieve, strain the mixture over a container.

Transfer the oat milk to a pitcher or Mason jar.

Cover the pitcher or jar, and transfer to the fridge to chill, for a minimum of 30 minutes.

Serve as needed.

*Serving size will depend on how you intend to use the milk

Pineapple Coconut Milk Oatmeal Smoothie

Two perfect flavors come together to create this smoothie that will remind you of sunny days spent at the beach.

Servings: 2

Total Time: 8hrs 15mins

Ingredients:

- ¼ cup uncooked old fashioned rolled oats
- 1½ tsp dried chia seeds
- 1 cup coconut milk, unsweetened
- ¼ cup low-fat Greek yogurt
- 1 cup fresh or canned pineapple chunks
- ½ tsp vanilla extract
- 1-2 tsp honey to sweeten

Directions:

In a food blender, combine the rolled oats with the chia seeds, and on high, process to a flour-like consistency.

Pour in the milk, and with a spoon, stir the oats and chia seeds sitting in the bottom of the blender jug.

Add the Greek yogurt, pineapple chunks, and vanilla extract and on high, blend to your desired level of smoothness.

Sweeten the smoothie with honey, blend once more, and transfer to a 2-cup container.

Transfer the smoothie to the fridge overnight.

The following day, remove from the fridge, shake well to combine and enjoy. If the smoothie is too thick, you can add a drop more milk, if needed, and shake to combine.

Pomegranate Blueberry Oatmeal Smoothie

Fruit-packed smoothies are healthy and delicious, but thanks to the oatmeal, this one is also super satisfying.

Servings: 2

Total Time: 8hrs 15mins

Ingredients:

- ¼ cup uncooked old fashioned oats
- 1½ tsp dried chia seeds
- ½ cup skim milk
- ½ cup pomegranate juice
- ¼ cup low-fat Greek yogurt
- 1 cup fresh blueberries
- ½ tsp vanilla extract
- 2-3 tsp honey

Directions:

In a food blender, combine the oats with the chia seeds and process at high speed to a flour-like consistency.

Add the milk and pomegranate juice to the blender, and with a spoon, stir the oat mixture sitting in the bottom of the blender jug.

Add the berries, and on high, blend to your preferred consistency.

Taste and add honey to sweeten. Blend once more and transfer to a 2-cup container.

Transfer the container to the fridge overnight to allow the oats and chia seeds to soften.

Remove from the fridge, and if too thick, add more pomegranate juice or milk and shake or blend to combine.

Strawberry Oatmeal Smoothie

This strawberry smoothie is the perfect after-school snack. What's more, your kids will love its sweet flavor.

Servings: 1

Total Time: 2mins

Ingredients:

- 1 cup frozen strawberries
- ¼ cup instant oats
- 2 cups milk
- 2 tbsp honey
- 1 tsp vanilla extract

Directions:

Add the frozen strawberries, instant oats, milk, honey, and vanilla extract to a food blender and process on high until smooth, for 30 seconds.

Serve and enjoy.

Vanilla Peppermint Overnight Oatmeal Smoothie

This fresh and minty overnight smoothie is well worth waking up to!

Servings: 1

Total Time: 8hrs 10mins

Ingredients:

- ½ cup rolled oats
- ¾ cup vanilla almond milk, unsweetened
- ½ tsp vanilla extract
- A pinch of salt
- ½ cup baby spinach
- 1 ripe banana, frozen
- 2 tbsp avocado, peeled and pitted
- 2-3 drops peppermint extract
- ½ - 1 tbsp sweetener of choice to taste

Directions:

The night before, in a food blender bowl, combine the oats with the almond milk, vanilla extract, and a pinch of salt. Stir to incorporate the ingredients, but do not process. Cover and transfer to the fridge overnight.

The following day, take the blender bowl out of the fridge and add the baby spinach, frozen banana, and avocado flesh.

At high speed, blend until creamy smooth. You may want to add extra vanilla almond milk to achieve your preferred consistency.

Add 2-3 drops of peppermint extract to taste, and blend for 2-3 seconds.

Taste and add sweetener if needed.

Transfer to a glass and enjoy.

Vanilla Oatmeal Latte

Unleash your inner barista and whip up this creamy coffee shop latte at home.

Servings: 2

Total Time: 8mins

Ingredients:

- 2½ cups whole milk, divided
- ¼ tsp salt
- ⅛ tsp ground cinnamon
- 1 cup old fashioned oats
- 1 tsp vanilla extract
- 3 tbsp brown sugar
- 2-4 shots espresso
- Granola to serve, optional

Directions:

In a pan, combine 1½ cups of milk, salt, and ground cinnamon and bring to a low boil.

Stir in the oats, and simmer until the milk is absorbed, for 3-5 minutes.

In the meantime, froth the remaining milk.

Stir in the vanilla extract and around ¾ of the frothy milk into the oats in the pan until creamy.

Remove the pan from the heat, and stir in the brown sugar followed by the remaining frothy milk.

Pour the latte into 2 coffee mugs, and top each one with espresso shots (to taste) and a sprinkling of granola.

Author's Afterthoughts

I would like to express my deepest thanks to you, the reader, for making this investment in one my books. I cherish the thought of bringing the love of cooking into your home.

With so much choice out there, I am grateful you decided to Purch this book and read it from beginning to end.

Please let me know by submitting an Amazon review if you enjoyed this book and found it contained valuable information to help you in your culinary endeavors. Please take a few minutes to express your opinion freely and honestly. This will help others make an informed decision on purchasing and provide me with valuable feedback.

Thank you for taking the time to review!

Christina Tosch

About the Author

Christina Tosch is a successful chef and renowned cookbook author from Long Grove, Illinois. She majored in Liberal Arts at Trinity International University and decided to pursue her passion of cooking when she applied to the world renowned Le Cordon Bleu culinary school in Paris, France. The school was lucky to recognize the immense talent of this chef and she excelled in her courses, particularly Haute Cuisine. This skill was recognized and rewarded by several highly regarded Chicago restaurants, where she was offered the prestigious position of head chef.

Christina and her family live in a spacious home in the Chicago area and she loves to grow her own vegetables and herbs in the garden she lovingly cultivates on her sprawling estate. Her and her husband have two beautiful children, 3 cats, 2 dogs and a parakeet they call Jasper. When Christina is not hard at work creating beautiful meals for Chicago's elite, she is hard at work writing engaging e-books of which she has sold over 1500.

Make sure to keep an eye out for her latest books that offer helpful tips, clear instructions and witty anecdotes that will bring a smile to your face as you read!

Printed in Great Britain
by Amazon